MW01115181

The Gospel of Mary

"Revelations of Mary: A Journey to Spiritual Enlightenment and Liberation"

Emily K Patel

Forbidden Mantra Press

I. Introduction

- ☐ The setting and characters
- ☐ Mary's discourse with the disciples

II. Mary's Teaching

- ☐ The soul and its liberation
- ☐ The conflict between matter and spirit
- ☐ The nature of sin
- ☐ The importance of spiritual practice
- ☐ The promise of eternal life

III. Dialogue with the Disciples

- ☐ Peter's objection and Andrew's support
- ☐ Levi's confession and Jesus' response

- Matthew's misunderstanding and Mary's clarification
- The disciples' grief and Jesus' encouragement

IV. The Vision of Mary

- Mary's ascent and encounter with the Savior
- Mary's report to the disciples
- The disciples' reaction and the end of the text

Note that the Gospel of Mary is a non-canonical text and the organization and content may vary depending on the translation and interpretation.

I. Introduction

The setting and characters

The Gospel of Mary is a Gnostic gospel that is believed to have been written in the early 2nd century CE, although the original text has not survived and only fragments of it remain. The text presents itself as a dialogue between the risen Christ and his disciples, focusing on Mary Magdalene's teachings and visions. The setting of the text is not explicitly stated, but it is assumed to take place in the aftermath of Jesus' crucifixion and resurrection.

The characters in the Gospel of Mary include:

1. Mary Magdalene: She is presented as a prominent disciple and leader among the followers of Jesus, who is given special insight into the spiritual teachings of Christ.

2. Peter: He is portrayed as a skeptical and sometimes confrontational figure, who challenges Mary's authority and her teachings.

3. Andrew: He is portrayed as a more sympathetic figure than Peter, who supports Mary and her teachings.

4. Levi: He is a disciple who confesses his doubts and sins to the group, and receives reassurance from Jesus.

5. Matthew: He is portrayed as a disciple who is confused by Mary's teachings, and requires further clarification.

6. The risen Christ: He appears to the disciples after his resurrection and engages in a dialogue with them, providing additional teachings and insights.

The Gospel of Mary presents a unique perspective on the early Christian movement and its characters, emphasizing the importance of Mary Magdalene and her teachings, which were largely excluded from the canonical Gospels.

Mary's discourse with the disciples

Certainly, I'll be happy to provide some elaboration on Mary's discourse with the disciples in the Gospel of Mary.

The Gospel of Mary presents a dialogue between Mary Magdalene and the disciples of Jesus, where

Mary is portrayed as a spiritual teacher who is given special insight into the teachings of Christ. The discourse begins with Mary speaking to the disciples, encouraging them to have faith and focus on their spiritual growth.

Mary's discourse with the disciples in the Gospel of Mary covers a range of spiritual topics, including the nature of the soul, the importance of spiritual practice, the conflict between matter and spirit, and the promise of eternal life. Some of the key themes that emerge from Mary's discourse include:

1. The liberation of the soul: Mary emphasizes the importance of freeing oneself from the constraints of the material world, and focusing on the growth of the soul. She describes the soul as being held captive by the material world, and encourages the disciples to seek spiritual liberation.

2. The conflict between matter and spirit: Mary explains that the material world is a source of suffering, and that the spirit must be freed from the constraints of the body in order to achieve spiritual growth. She argues that the material world is a source of temptation, and that spiritual discipline is necessary in order to resist its influence.

3. The nature of sin: Mary offers a unique perspective on the nature of sin, arguing that it arises from ignorance and misunderstanding, rather than from intentional wrongdoing. She suggests that the disciples must strive to overcome their ignorance in order to avoid sin.

4. The importance of spiritual practice: Mary emphasizes the importance of spiritual practice, including prayer, fasting, and contemplation, as a means of achieving

spiritual growth. She argues that spiritual practice is necessary in order to overcome the influence of the material world, and to achieve a higher state of consciousness.

Overall, Mary's discourse with the disciples in the Gospel of Mary presents a unique perspective on the nature of spirituality and the importance of spiritual practice, and provides valuable insights into the spiritual teachings of the early Christian movement.

Commentary:

Title: A Profound Discourse Unveiled: Mary's Encounter with the Disciples

Introduction: In the realm of ancient biblical narratives, certain passages have transcended time to become timeless tales of inspiration and enlightenment. One such instance can be found in the profound discourse between Mary and the disciples. As the setting and characters converge, this captivating exchange captivates our imagination, revealing layers of meaning and offering valuable insights. Let us delve into this remarkable encounter and explore its significance.

The Setting and Characters: The scene unfolds against the backdrop of an era permeated with profound spiritual occurrences. The disciples, fervent followers of Jesus Christ, find themselves grappling with the aftermath of his crucifixion. Emotions run high, with a mixture of grief, confusion, and uncertainty clouding their hearts and minds. It is in this state of vulnerability that

Mary, a steadfast and devoted disciple, steps forward to converse with them.

Mary's Discourse with the Disciples: Mary's discourse with the disciples is a poignant and transformative moment. Through her words, she imparts wisdom, reassurance, and a renewed sense of purpose. Her gentle yet resolute demeanor sets the stage for a profound exchange of ideas and emotions.

As the disciples express their anguish and confusion, Mary listens intently, recognizing the depth of their pain. She does not dismiss their emotions but rather acknowledges their validity. In her response, Mary shares her own experiences and insights, drawing upon her unwavering faith and connection with Jesus.

With heartfelt conviction, Mary encourages the disciples to embrace hope and trust in the divine plan. She reminds them of Jesus' teachings, emphasizing the importance of perseverance and unwavering faith. Her words carry a profound sense of comfort, urging the disciples to move beyond their grief and uncertainty and embrace the transformative power of love and spiritual truth.

Through this discourse, Mary's role transcends that of a mere messenger. She becomes a beacon of strength, compassion, and guidance, symbolizing the indomitable spirit that lies within each of us. Her words ignite a spark within the disciples, rejuvenating their commitment to carry forth Jesus' message and purpose.

Significance and Lessons: Mary's discourse with the disciples holds timeless significance, resonating with readers and seekers of truth across generations. It exemplifies the power of compassion, understanding, and resilience in times of turmoil. Her unwavering faith and ability to channel her grief into transformative energy offer a profound lesson in finding strength in vulnerability.

Furthermore, this discourse highlights the importance of communal support and dialogue. Mary's willingness to engage in conversation with the disciples creates a space for healing and growth. It demonstrates that in times of crisis, sharing our burdens and seeking solace in one another can lead to profound revelations and spiritual renewal.

In conclusion, Mary's discourse with the disciples stands as a testament to the power of faith, compassion, and perseverance. It reminds us that even in the darkest of times, there is potential for hope and transformation. As we reflect upon this extraordinary encounter, let us draw inspiration from Mary's unwavering conviction and strive to embody the qualities that can help us navigate the complexities of our own lives.

II. Mary's Teaching

The soul and its liberation

In the Gospel of Mary, the soul is presented as an essential component of the human being, which is often held captive by the material world. Mary argues that the soul is trapped within the material body, and that its liberation is necessary in order to achieve spiritual growth and enlightenment. Mary emphasizes the importance of spiritual discipline as a means of liberating the soul from the material world. She suggests that spiritual practices such as prayer, fasting, and contemplation can help to free the soul from the constraints of the body, and allow it to achieve a higher state of consciousness.

Mary's teachings on the liberation of the soul are closely linked to the Gnostic belief in the separation between the material world and the divine realm. Gnostics believed that the material world was created by a flawed and inferior deity, and that the true divine realm was separate from the material world. According to this view, the liberation of the soul involves freeing it from the influence of the material world, and allowing it to ascend to the divine realm.

Mary's teachings on the liberation of the soul are also closely linked to the idea of spiritual rebirth or transformation. She suggests that the process of spiritual growth involves a kind of death and rebirth, in which the old self is shed in order to make way for the new self. Mary suggests that this process of transformation is necessary in order to achieve spiritual liberation and to live a life in accordance with the divine will.

Overall, the concept of the soul and its liberation in the Gospel of Mary emphasizes the importance of spiritual growth and the pursuit of enlightenment, and provides valuable insights into the Gnostic view of the relationship between the material world and the divine realm.

The Conflict Between Matter and Spirit

The conflict between matter and spirit in the Gospel of Mary

The Gospel of Mary presents a Gnostic perspective that views the material world as a source of suffering and limitation, and emphasizes the importance of transcending the material world in order to achieve spiritual growth and enlightenment. Mary argues that the material world is a source of temptation, and that the pursuit of material desires can lead to spiritual decay and moral corruption.

According to Mary, the conflict between matter and spirit is fundamental to human existence, and can only be resolved through spiritual discipline and the pursuit of enlightenment. She suggests that the body and the material world are often at odds with the spirit, and that the spirit must be liberated from the constraints of the body in order to achieve spiritual growth.

Mary emphasizes the importance of spiritual practice as a means of overcoming the influence of the material world. She suggests that practices such as prayer, fasting, and contemplation can help to free the spirit from the influence of the body, and allow it to achieve a higher state of consciousness. She argues that spiritual discipline is necessary in order to resist the temptations of the material world, and to achieve a state of spiritual purity and enlightenment.

Mary's teachings on the conflict between matter and spirit are closely linked to the Gnostic belief in the separation between the material world and the divine realm. Gnostics believed that the material world was created by a flawed and inferior deity, and that the true divine realm was separate from the material world. According to this view, the conflict between matter and spirit is seen as a fundamental aspect of the human condition, which can only be resolved through the pursuit of spiritual enlightenment and the liberation of the spirit from the constraints of the material world.

Overall, Mary's teachings on the conflict between matter and spirit emphasize the importance of spiritual discipline and the pursuit of enlightenment, and provide valuable insights into the Gnostic view of the relationship between the material world and the divine realm.

Commentary:

Title: Navigating the Conflict Between Matter and Spirit: A Commentary

Introduction: The conflict between matter and spirit has long been a subject of contemplation and philosophical inquiry. It is a fundamental dichotomy that explores the tension between the physical realm and the intangible aspects of human existence. This commentary delves into this age-old conflict, examining its implications, complexities, and potential resolutions.

The Clash of Matter and Spirit: The conflict between matter and spirit arises from the inherent duality of human nature. On one hand, we are bound by the material world, characterized by physical bodies, tangible objects, and the limitations of time and space. On the other hand, we possess an inner realm of consciousness, emotions, thoughts, and the quest for transcendence.

At its core, this conflict revolves around the struggle between the transient nature of the physical world and the eternal aspirations of the human spirit. Our material desires, attachments, and worldly pursuits often seem at odds with our yearning for meaning, purpose, and spiritual growth. This clash can lead to a profound sense of disconnection, existential crises, and a search for harmony.

Seeking Balance and Integration: While the conflict between matter and spirit may appear insurmountable, seeking balance and integration becomes a pathway to resolution. Instead of viewing them as opposing forces, recognizing the interconnectedness and interdependence of matter and spirit allows for a holistic perspective.

The material world, with its sensory experiences and tangible manifestations, provides the context for spiritual growth and self-realization. It is through our interactions with the physical realm that we gain wisdom, develop virtues, and cultivate compassion. Simultaneously, acknowledging and nurturing our spiritual dimension empowers us to transcend the limitations of matter and access higher states of consciousness.

Transcending the Conflict: Transcending the conflict between matter and spirit involves a transformative journey of self-discovery and inner exploration. This journey requires introspection, mindfulness, and a willingness to delve into the depths of our being.

One approach to resolving this conflict is by aligning our actions and intentions with spiritual values. By consciously infusing our daily lives with qualities such as love, kindness, integrity, and selflessness, we bridge the gap between matter and spirit. This integration fosters a sense of coherence, where our material existence becomes a vehicle for spiritual expression.

Another avenue is through practices that promote inner stillness and contemplation, such as meditation, prayer, or reflection. These practices cultivate awareness, allowing us to transcend the limitations of the physical world and connect with the essence of our being. In these moments of transcendence, the conflict between matter and spirit dissolves, revealing a deeper sense of unity and interconnectedness.

Conclusion: The conflict between matter and spirit is a profound existential challenge faced by individuals throughout history. While the tension between the two realms is undeniable, it is through seeking balance, integration, and transcendence that we can navigate this conflict and find harmony. By embracing both the material and spiritual aspects of our existence, we unlock the potential for personal growth, self-realization, and a more profound understanding of our place in the universe.

The nature of sin

The Gospel of Mary presents a Gnostic perspective on sin, which differs from the traditional Christian view in a number of ways. While traditional

Christianity views sin as a transgression of God's law, Gnostic beliefs focus more on the nature of the material world and its negative influence on the human spirit.

According to the Gospel of Mary, sin is not simply a matter of breaking God's commandments, but is rather a state of being that results from being trapped in the material world. Mary argues that the material world is corrupt and imperfect, and that its influence can lead to spiritual decay and moral corruption.

Mary suggests that sin is a natural consequence of living in the material world, and that it can only be overcome through spiritual discipline and the pursuit of enlightenment. She emphasizes the importance of freeing the spirit from the constraints of the body and the material world, in order to achieve spiritual purity and enlightenment.

Mary also suggests that the pursuit of material desires is a source of sin, and that the pursuit of spiritual growth and enlightenment is the key to overcoming sin. She argues that the pursuit of material desires can lead to spiritual decay and moral corruption, and that only by focusing on the pursuit of spiritual growth and enlightenment can the human spirit be liberated from the negative influence of the material world.

Overall, the Gospel of Mary presents a view of sin that is closely linked to the Gnostic view of the relationship between the material world and the divine realm. Mary's teachings emphasize the importance of spiritual discipline and the pursuit of enlightenment, and provide valuable insights into the Gnostic perspective on the nature of sin and its role in the human condition.

Commentary:

Title: Illuminating the Nature of Sin: Insights from the Nag Hammadi Texts of Mary Magdalene

Introduction: The Nag Hammadi texts, including the poignant writings attributed to Mary Magdalene, provide an alternative perspective on the nature of sin. This commentary explores the profound insights offered by these texts, shedding light on the complexities and transformative potential of sin as portrayed through the lens of Mary Magdalene's teachings.

Challenging Traditional Notions: Mary Magdalene's teachings, as found in the Nag Hammadi texts, challenge the conventional understanding of sin as solely a moral transgression. Instead, they invite us to embrace a more nuanced comprehension of sin, one that encompasses not only external actions but also the internal realms of consciousness, thoughts, and intentions.

Sin as Ignorance and Separation: According to Mary Magdalene's teachings, sin is often rooted in ignorance and the illusion of separation. It is a state of disconnection from our true nature, the divine, and the interconnectedness of all beings. Sin emerges when we lose sight of our inherent divinity and become entangled in ego-driven desires, attachments, and distorted perceptions.

In this context, sin is not solely a punitive concept but an invitation to awaken from our state of ignorance and reunite with the deeper truths that reside within us. It is a call to transcend the illusions of separation and recognize the inherent oneness of all existence.

The Transformative Power of Sin: Rather than being condemned or suppressed, sin, as understood by Mary Magdalene, holds transformative potential. It serves as a catalyst for spiritual growth, self-reflection, and the realization of our divine nature. Sin, when consciously acknowledged and embraced, becomes a gateway to self-awareness, humility, and a deeper understanding of our interconnectedness.

Through the transformative process, sin can be transmuted into wisdom, compassion, and a renewed commitment to living in alignment with the divine principles of love and harmony. It is through the acknowledgment, forgiveness, and integration of our own sins that we can extend compassion and forgiveness to others, fostering collective healing and spiritual evolution.

Embracing Divine Grace and Love: The Nag Hammadi texts of Mary Magdalene also emphasize the importance of divine grace and unconditional love in the context of sin. They suggest that our inherent divine essence transcends any wrongdoing, offering the opportunity for redemption, forgiveness, and liberation from the burdens of sin.

By opening ourselves to receive divine grace and cultivating self-compassion, we can embark on a journey of healing and restoration. Mary Magdalene's teachings encourage us to tap into the transformative power of love, both within ourselves and in our relationships with others, fostering a deeper understanding of sin as a catalyst for growth rather than a cause for condemnation.

Conclusion: The Nag Hammadi texts attributed to Mary Magdalene invite us to reframe our understanding of sin, embracing a more expansive and transformative perspective. They guide us towards recognizing sin as a consequence of ignorance and separation, while also illuminating the potential for redemption, self-realization, and the awakening of love and compassion.

Through these teachings, we are encouraged to embark on a personal journey of self-discovery, embracing divine grace, and embodying unconditional love. By integrating these insights into our lives, we can navigate the complexities of sin with wisdom, humility, and an unwavering commitment to the path of spiritual growth and interconnectedness.

The importance of spiritual practice

The Gospel of Mary emphasizes the importance of spiritual practice as a means of achieving spiritual growth and enlightenment. Mary suggests that spiritual practice is necessary in order to free the spirit from the constraints of the material world, and to achieve a higher state of consciousness.

Mary emphasizes several spiritual practices that can help individuals to achieve spiritual growth and enlightenment. These practices include prayer, fasting, and contemplation. Through these practices, individuals can develop a deeper connection to the divine realm and gain a greater understanding of the spiritual nature of reality. Mary also emphasizes the importance of spiritual discipline in the pursuit of enlightenment. She suggests that individuals must cultivate a sense of inner discipline and focus in order to overcome the negative influence of the material world and achieve spiritual purity.

In addition to individual spiritual practices, Mary also emphasizes the importance of spiritual community. She suggests that individuals should seek out the company of other spiritual seekers in order to gain support and encouragement on their spiritual journey.

Overall, the Gospel of Mary emphasizes the importance of spiritual practice in the pursuit of spiritual growth and enlightenment. Mary's teachings provide valuable insights into the Gnostic view of the relationship between the material world and the divine realm, and emphasize the importance of cultivating a deeper spiritual connection in order to overcome the negative influence of the material world and achieve spiritual purity.

Commentary:

Title: Rediscovering Mary Magdalene: Insights from the Nag Hammadi Texts

Introduction: The Nag Hammadi texts have provided a valuable glimpse into the teachings and wisdom of Mary Magdalene, a figure often obscured by historical narratives. This commentary explores the significance of Mary Magdalene's portrayal in these texts, highlighting her role as a spiritual leader, a bearer of divine knowledge, and an embodiment of feminine wisdom.

Reclaiming Mary Magdalene's Narrative: The Nag Hammadi texts offer an opportunity to challenge the traditional depiction of Mary Magdalene and reclaim her rightful place as a prominent figure in early Christian and Gnostic traditions. These texts present her not merely as a repentant sinner but as a disciple, confidante, and teacher, who shares profound insights into the nature of spirituality and the path to self-realization.

Spiritual Authority and Discipleship: Mary Magdalene emerges in the Nag Hammadi texts as a spiritual authority in her own right. She is portrayed as one who received direct teachings from Jesus and possessed deep understanding and experiential knowledge of spiritual truths. Her status as a disciple and her close connection with Jesus challenge the patriarchal narratives that have marginalized women's roles in religious history.

Moreover, Mary Magdalene's discipleship transcends traditional hierarchical structures, emphasizing the importance of direct personal experience and inner transformation. She embodies the essence of an enlightened teacher, guiding others towards self-discovery and union with the divine.

Feminine Wisdom and Divine Sophia: The Nag Hammadi texts portray Mary Magdalene as a vessel of feminine wisdom, carrying the embodiment of the divine Sophia—the feminine aspect of the divine presence. Through her teachings, Mary Magdalene reveals the inherent power and importance of the feminine in spiritual growth and understanding.

Her embodiment of Sophia exemplifies the recognition of the sacred balance between masculine and feminine energies, highlighting the need for harmony and integration in spiritual pursuits. Mary Magdalene's teachings resonate with a deep reverence for the divine feminine, urging individuals to honor and embrace this aspect within themselves and the world around them.

Gnosis and Inner Revelation: Central to Mary Magdalene's teachings in the Nag Hammadi texts is the concept of gnosis—the direct experiential knowledge of spiritual truths. She encourages individuals to embark on an inward journey of self-discovery, transcending external dogmas and embracing personal revelation.

Mary Magdalene's emphasis on gnosis underscores the significance of personal and mystical experiences in spiritual growth. She invites seekers to cultivate a deep connection with their inner selves and the divine, recognizing that true wisdom arises from direct communion with the divine source.

Relevance and Inspiration Today: The insights and teachings of Mary Magdalene from the Nag Hammadi texts continue to resonate and inspire seekers of truth in contemporary times. Her role as a spiritual leader, the embodiment of feminine wisdom, and her emphasis on personal revelation and inner transformation offer a profound and relevant framework for spiritual seekers today.

By reclaiming and honoring Mary Magdalene's voice, we expand our understanding of the diverse spiritual traditions and the vital role women have played throughout history. Her teachings serve as a reminder of the inclusive, empowering, and transformative potential of spirituality for all individuals, regardless of gender or societal expectations.

Conclusion: The Nag Hammadi texts have illuminated the figure of Mary Magdalene, revealing her as a visionary teacher, disciple, and bearer of feminine wisdom. Her teachings emphasize the importance of personal revelation, inner transformation, and the recognition of the divine feminine. As we engage with Mary Magdalene's teachings, we are invited to embrace the depths of our own spirituality, embody wisdom, and honor the sacred balance between masculine and feminine energies in our spiritual journey.

\The promise of eternal life

The Gospel of Mary suggests that the promise of
eternal life is available to those who achieve
spiritual enlightenment and liberation from the
constraints of the material world. Mary argues that

the material world is corrupt and imperfect, and that the pursuit of material desires can lead to spiritual decay and moral corruption.

According to Mary, the pursuit of spiritual growth and enlightenment is the key to achieving eternal life. She suggests that the spirit can be liberated from the constraints of the body and the material world through spiritual practice and discipline. By achieving spiritual purity and enlightenment, individuals can attain a state of consciousness that is free from the limitations and imperfections of the material world.

Mary suggests that eternal life is not simply a matter of living forever, but is rather a state of being that transcends the limitations of the material world. She argues that eternal life is a state of consciousness in which the individual is united with the divine realm, and is free from the negative influence of the material world.

Mary's teachings on the promise of eternal life are closely linked to the Gnostic view of the relationship between the material world and the divine realm. Gnostics believed that the material world was created by a

flawed and inferior deity, and that the true divine realm was separate from the material world. According to this view, the pursuit of spiritual growth and enlightenment was seen as the key to achieving eternal life and uniting with the divine realm.

Overall, the Gospel of Mary provides valuable insights into the Gnostic view of the promise of eternal life, and emphasizes the importance of spiritual practice and discipline in achieving spiritual enlightenment and liberation from the constraints of the material world.

Commentary:

Title: Mary Magdalene's Revelation: The Promise of Eternal Life in the Nag Hammadi Texts

Introduction: The Nag Hammadi texts offer profound insights into the teachings of Mary Magdalene, shedding light on her role as a bearer of divine knowledge and her profound understanding of the promise of eternal life. This commentary explores the significance of Mary Magdalene's teachings in relation to the concept of eternal life, highlighting her transformative message of spiritual liberation and transcendence.

Reimagining Eternal Life: Mary Magdalene's teachings challenge traditional notions of eternal life as a distant future reward or a posthumous existence. Instead, she unveils a deeper understanding, emphasizing that eternal life is not confined to a distant realm but is a present and transformative reality that can be accessed within the depths of our being.

The Mystical Journey: Mary Magdalene's teachings emphasize the mystical journey of self-discovery and inner transformation as the pathway to experiencing eternal life. She invites seekers to transcend the limitations of the ego and embrace a direct connection with the divine, unveiling the eternal essence that resides within each individual.

Through practices such as meditation, contemplation, and inner stillness, one can pierce through the illusions of time and space, entering into a timeless realm where the promise of eternal life becomes a tangible experience. Mary

Magdalene's teachings empower individuals to seek this transformative connection with the divine, transcending the boundaries of the physical world.

Union with the Divine: Central to Mary Magdalene's teachings is the notion of union with the divine. She emphasizes that eternal life is not a separate existence but a deepening communion with the divine presence that transcends temporal limitations. By recognizing the inherent divinity within oneself and aligning with the divine source, individuals can partake in the eternal nature of the divine and experience a profound sense of oneness.

Mary Magdalene's teachings echo the Gnostic understanding that the spark of the divine resides within each person, and through gnosis (direct experiential knowledge), one can attain union with the divine essence. This union brings about a transformative shift in consciousness, transcending the confines of mortality and offering a taste of the eternal.

Freedom from Cycle of Rebirth: Another aspect of Mary Magdalene's teachings on eternal life is the liberation from the cycle of rebirth. She reveals that through the realization of one's divine nature and the attainment of gnosis, individuals can transcend the repetitive cycle of birth and death, liberating themselves from the limitations of the physical realm.

Mary Magdalene's teachings offer a profound message of liberation, encouraging individuals to free themselves from attachments, desires, and the illusion of separateness. By embracing the eternal essence within, one can transcend the karmic cycle and attain a state of spiritual freedom.

Living in the Light of Eternity: Mary Magdalene's teachings on eternal life invite individuals to live in the light of eternity in the present moment. They call for a shift in consciousness, urging seekers to embody qualities such as love, compassion, and wisdom that align with the eternal essence within.

By aligning our thoughts, actions, and intentions with the eternal truth, we participate in the unfolding of eternal life in our daily lives. Mary Magdalene's teachings encourage individuals to embrace a spiritual perspective, viewing life as an opportunity to embody the eternal qualities of the divine and contribute to the collective awakening of humanity.

Conclusion: Mary Magdalene's teachings in the Nag Hammadi texts illuminate the profound promise of eternal life. Through her wisdom, she guides seekers towards a transformative journey of self-discovery, union with the divine, and liberation from the cycle of rebirth. Her teachings emphasize the present and experiential nature of eternal life, inviting individuals to embody the eternal essence within and live in alignment with divine

III. Dialogue with the Disciples

Peter's objection and Andrew's support

In the Gospel of Mary, after Mary delivers her discourse on spiritual matters, Peter objects to her teachings. He questions her authority to teach, as well as the validity of her teachings, and suggests that the disciples should not believe her.

However, Andrew, another disciple, supports Mary and defends her teachings. He argues that Mary has received special knowledge and insight from the Lord that the other disciples have not. He encourages the other disciples to listen to Mary's words and consider their validity, rather than dismissing them outright.

Peter's objection and Andrew's support illustrate the tension and disagreements that could arise within the early Christian community over matters of theology and authority. Peter represents a more traditional perspective, rooted in Jewish law and tradition, while Andrew represents a more open-minded and inclusive perspective, willing to consider alternative viewpoints and sources of knowledge.

The conflict between Peter and Andrew over Mary's teachings also highlights the importance of critical thinking and discernment in matters of faith. The Gospel of Mary suggests that spiritual teachings should not be accepted blindly, but should be evaluated based on their truthfulness and their ability to help individuals achieve spiritual growth and enlightenment.

Overall, the objection raised by Peter and the support offered by Andrew provide valuable insights into the complexities of early Christian theology and the diversity of opinions and beliefs that existed within the community.

Commentary:

Title: Mary Magdalene and the Voices of Peter's Objection and Andrew's Support: A Commentary on the Nag Hammadi Texts

Introduction: The Nag Hammadi texts offer a unique perspective on the interactions between Mary Magdalene and the disciples, particularly focusing on Peter's objection and Andrew's support. This commentary explores the significance of these contrasting voices, shedding light on the dynamics surrounding Mary Magdalene's role and the unfolding spiritual revelations within the text.

Peter's Objection: Peter's objection, as depicted in the Nag Hammadi texts, reflects a prevailing societal and cultural context that marginalized women and questioned their authority in religious matters. Peter's objection to Mary Magdalene's role and teachings highlights the resistance to accepting her as an equal spiritual leader.

Peter's objection may stem from a combination of ingrained biases, fear of change, and adherence to hierarchical structures. It serves as a reminder of the challenges faced by women seeking to assert their spiritual authority within patriarchal systems.

Andrew's Support: In contrast to Peter's objection, Andrew's support for Mary Magdalene showcases a more inclusive and accepting perspective. Andrew recognizes the spiritual wisdom and depth of Mary Magdalene's teachings, embracing her as a valuable contributor to the collective spiritual journey.

Andrew's support signifies the potential for growth, openness, and the recognition of the inherent worth and spiritual insight that women, like Mary Magdalene, possess. His stance reflects a willingness to challenge societal norms and embrace a more egalitarian approach to spirituality.

Unveiling Divine Wisdom: The interaction between Mary Magdalene, Peter, and Andrew represents a larger narrative within the Nag Hammadi texts—one that illuminates the tension between traditional structures and the emergence of a more expansive understanding of divine wisdom. Mary Magdalene's presence challenges the established order, inviting a reevaluation of gender roles and spiritual authority.

Her teachings emphasize the importance of direct personal experience, inner transformation, and the pursuit of gnosis (direct experiential knowledge). Mary Magdalene's wisdom serves as a conduit for unveiling divine truths that transcend societal constructs and expand the possibilities for spiritual growth.

The Relevance Today: The voices of Peter's objection and Andrew's support in the Nag Hammadi texts hold relevance in contemporary conversations surrounding gender equality, spiritual authority, and inclusivity. They prompt us to examine our own biases and question the structures that may limit the full expression of spiritual wisdom.

The encounter between Mary Magdalene, Peter, and Andrew invites us to recognize and challenge societal norms that hinder the recognition of diverse voices and perspectives in spiritual discourse. It encourages us to create spaces where the spiritual insights of all individuals, irrespective of gender, are honored and valued.

Embracing a Multifaceted Spirituality: The Nag Hammadi texts, through the interplay of Peter's objection and Andrew's support, beckon us to embrace a multifaceted spirituality that transcends gender stereotypes and embraces the inherent wisdom within all beings. They remind us of the transformative potential that arises when we honor and integrate diverse voices and perspectives into our spiritual journeys.

Conclusion: The portrayal of Peter's objection and Andrew's support in the Nag Hammadi texts surrounding Mary Magdalene signifies a pivotal moment in challenging gender biases and redefining spiritual authority. It invites us to reflect on the limitations imposed by societal constructs and embrace a more inclusive, egalitarian approach to spirituality—one that recognizes the inherent worth and wisdom of individuals like Mary Magdalene.

By embracing the transformative messages within the Nag Hammadi texts, we are called to create spaces where diverse spiritual voices are valued, fostering a collective journey towards a more inclusive and enlightened understanding of spirituality.

Levi's confession and Jesus' response

In the Gospel of Mary, Levi, also known as Matthew, confesses his doubts and fears to the other disciples after Mary's discourse. He expresses uncertainty about the validity of their teachings and the possibility of achieving spiritual enlightenment. Jesus responds to Levi's confession by offering words of comfort and encouragement. He acknowledges Levi's doubts and fears, but emphasizes the importance of persevering in the pursuit of spiritual growth and enlightenment. Jesus suggests that the path to spiritual enlightenment is not easy, but requires discipline, dedication, and faith.

Jesus also offers a metaphor to illustrate the importance of spiritual perseverance. He compares the pursuit of spiritual growth to the act of fishing, suggesting that just as fishermen must persist in their efforts to catch fish, so too must individuals persist in their efforts to achieve spiritual enlightenment.

Jesus' response to Levi's confession provides valuable insights into the nature of spiritual growth and the challenges that individuals may face on their journey. His words emphasize the importance of perseverance, discipline, and faith in the pursuit of spiritual enlightenment, and suggest that doubts and fears are natural and should be acknowledged and addressed.

Commentary:

Title: Mary Magdalene and the Profound Encounter: Levi's Confession and Jesus' Response in the Nag Hammadi Texts

Introduction: Within the Nag Hammadi texts, an encounter between Mary Magdalene, Levi, and Jesus unfolds, culminating in Levi's confession and

Jesus' response. This commentary explores the significance of this powerful interaction, shedding light on the themes of forgiveness, transformation, and the potential for redemption as depicted in the writings attributed to Mary Magdalene.

Levi's Confession: Levi's confession within the Nag Hammadi texts reflects a profound moment of self-awareness and vulnerability. It showcases the universal human experience of recognizing one's own shortcomings, mistakes, and the desire for spiritual healing and redemption.

Levi's willingness to lay bare his faults and seek forgiveness highlights the transformative power of confession as a gateway to self-transcendence and spiritual growth. His confession serves as a catalyst for inner transformation and a reminder that acknowledgment of our imperfections can lead to a deeper connection with the divine.

Jesus' Response: Jesus' response to Levi's confession in the Nag Hammadi texts exemplifies the essence of compassion, forgiveness, and unconditional love. His acceptance of Levi's confession without judgment or condemnation embodies the transformative nature of divine grace and the potential for redemption.

Jesus' response underscores the core teachings attributed to Mary Magdalene, emphasizing the inherent worth and dignity of every individual, regardless of their past actions. His compassion and forgiveness offer a profound invitation for personal and spiritual renewal, inspiring individuals to embrace their capacity for transformation and embark on a path of healing.

Forgiveness and Liberation: The encounter between Mary Magdalene, Levi, and Jesus within the Nag Hammadi texts illuminates the liberating power of forgiveness. It reveals that forgiveness is not solely an act bestowed by a higher authority, but a transformative process that enables individuals to liberate themselves from the burdens of guilt, shame, and past mistakes.

Mary Magdalene's teachings, as conveyed through this encounter, emphasize the importance of self-forgiveness and the recognition that divine love and grace are available to all who seek redemption. This profound message resonates with the potential for healing and liberation that lies within each individual, fostering a deeper understanding of one's inherent capacity for transformation.

The Relevance Today: The encounter between Mary Magdalene, Levi, and Jesus holds great relevance in contemporary times. It serves as a powerful reminder of the transformative potential inherent in acknowledging our shortcomings, seeking forgiveness, and embracing the divine love and grace available to us all.

In a world often burdened by judgment, shame, and unforgiving attitudes, this encounter calls us to cultivate a culture of compassion, forgiveness, and acceptance. It invites us to recognize the transformative power of vulnerability and self-reflection, fostering an environment where individuals can find healing, redemption, and the freedom to embark on a path of personal and spiritual growth.

Conclusion: The encounter between Mary Magdalene, Levi, and Jesus, as depicted in the Nag Hammadi texts, offers profound insights into the themes of confession, forgiveness, and transformation. It highlights the inherent potential for redemption and liberation within the human experience.

By embracing the transformative messages conveyed through this encounter, we are called to extend compassion, forgiveness, and acceptance to ourselves and others. Mary Magdalene's teachings remind us of the transformative power of vulnerability, self-reflection, and divine grace, inspiring us to embark on a journey of healing and spiritual growth.

Matthew's misunderstanding and Mary's clarification

In the Gospel of Mary, Matthew expresses his confusion and misunderstanding about some of the teachings that Mary has shared with the disciples. He asks for clarification on a particular point, and Mary responds by providing a more detailed explanation.

Mary's clarification highlights the importance of interpreting spiritual teachings correctly and avoiding misunderstandings that can lead to confusion and misguidance. She emphasizes the need to approach spiritual teachings with an open mind and a willingness to seek understanding, rather than assuming that one already knows the answer.

Mary's response also underscores the importance of dialogue and discussion in matters of faith. Rather than dismissing Matthew's confusion or leaving him with incomplete understanding, she engages in a conversation with him, offering additional insights and clarifications.

Overall, Matthew's misunderstanding and Mary's clarification illustrate the importance of critical thinking, open-mindedness, and dialogue in matters of faith. They highlight the need to approach spiritual teachings with humility and a willingness to learn, and underscore the importance of seeking clarification when confusion arises.

Commentary:

Title: Mary Magdalene's Clarity: Matthew's Misunderstanding and Mary's Clarification in the Nag Hammadi Texts

Introduction: In the Nag Hammadi texts, an exchange between Mary Magdalene, Matthew, and other disciples unfolds, highlighting Matthew's misunderstanding and Mary's role in providing clarification. This commentary delves into the significance of this encounter, emphasizing the role of Mary Magdalene as a source of wisdom and insight, and the importance of transcending limited perceptions in spiritual understanding.

Matthew's Misunderstanding: Matthew's misunderstanding within the Nag Hammadi texts symbolizes the limitations of a rigid and literal interpretation of spiritual teachings. His inability to grasp the deeper meaning of Mary Magdalene's words reflects the challenges of fixed belief systems and the resistance to embracing a broader, more nuanced understanding.

Matthew's misunderstanding serves as a reminder of the importance of openness, humility, and a willingness to question preconceived notions in the pursuit of spiritual truth. It highlights the potential pitfalls of clinging to dogma without engaging in deeper reflection and exploration.

Mary's Clarification: Mary Magdalene's role in providing clarification showcases her wisdom and insight as a spiritual leader. Her response to Matthew's misunderstanding demonstrates her ability to discern the deeper layers of truth and to convey them with clarity and compassion.

Mary's clarification invites the disciples, including Matthew, to move beyond surface-level interpretations and engage in a more profound exploration of the teachings. Her guidance encourages them to seek a direct and personal experience of the divine, transcending limited understanding and embracing a more expansive perspective.

Transcending Limited Perceptions: The encounter between Mary Magdalene, Matthew, and the other disciples in the Nag Hammadi texts highlights the importance of transcending limited perceptions in the pursuit of spiritual growth. It calls for a shift from a rigid, narrow-minded approach to a more open, inclusive, and nuanced understanding of spiritual truths.

Mary Magdalene's teachings emphasize the need for direct personal experience, inner transformation, and the cultivation of wisdom. Her role as a clarifying voice challenges the disciples to question their own assumptions, expand their consciousness, and embrace a deeper spiritual understanding that transcends superficial interpretations.

Relevance in Today's Spiritual Journey: The dynamics between Mary Magdalene, Matthew, and the other disciples in the Nag Hammadi texts hold great relevance in contemporary spiritual exploration. They remind us of the importance of remaining open-minded, receptive, and humble in our spiritual quest, avoiding the pitfalls of rigid beliefs and limited perspectives.

Mary Magdalene's role as a guide and clarifier inspires us to seek deeper insights, question established dogmas, and engage in personal reflection and inner transformation. Her teachings invite us to transcend limited perceptions, embrace a more expansive understanding of spirituality, and cultivate a direct, authentic connection with the divine.

Conclusion: The encounter between Mary Magdalene, Matthew, and the other disciples in the Nag Hammadi texts presents an invaluable lesson in spiritual understanding. Matthew's misunderstanding and Mary's clarification serve as reminders of the importance of transcending limited perceptions and embracing a more nuanced, expansive approach to spiritual truths.

Mary Magdalene's role as a source of wisdom and insight offers guidance for seekers on their spiritual journey, encouraging them to move beyond superficial interpretations and embrace a deeper, more experiential understanding of the divine. By following her example, we can cultivate a richer, more transformative spiritual path, transcending limitations and accessing profound insights that lead to personal growth and connection with the sacred.

The disciples' grief and Jesus' encouragement

In the Gospel of Mary, the disciples experience grief and sorrow after Jesus' departure from their midst. They express their sadness and despair, feeling lost without their teacher and unsure of how to continue on their spiritual path.

Jesus responds to their grief by offering words of encouragement and reassurance. He reminds them of their inner strength and resilience, and encourages them to continue on their spiritual journey, even in the face of adversity and challenge. Jesus' response to the disciples' grief highlights the importance of resilience and perseverance in matters of faith. He acknowledges their pain and sorrow, but reminds them of their ability to overcome difficulties and continue on their spiritual path. His words offer comfort and hope, reminding the disciples that they are not alone and that they can draw on their own inner resources to overcome obstacles and achieve spiritual growth.

Overall, the disciples' grief and Jesus' encouragement provide valuable insights into the challenges and rewards of the spiritual journey. They underscore the importance of resilience and perseverance in the face of adversity, and highlight the power of community and support in helping individuals navigate the ups and downs of the spiritual path.

Commentary:

Title: Mary Magdalene's Comfort: The Disciples' Grief and Jesus' Encouragement in the Nag Hammadi Texts

Introduction: In the Nag Hammadi texts, an emotionally charged moment unfolds as the disciples, including Mary Magdalene, experience deep grief following Jesus' departure. This commentary explores the significance of Mary Magdalene's role in comforting the disciples and Jesus' words of encouragement, highlighting the themes of hope, resilience, and the transformative power of love.

The Disciples' Grief: The disciples' grief depicted in the Nag Hammadi texts serves as a reflection of the profound loss they experienced upon Jesus' physical departure. Their sorrow underscores the depth of their connection to him and the impact of his teachings and presence in their lives.

This portrayal of grief humanizes the disciples, emphasizing the complex range of emotions they experienced in the wake of Jesus' absence. It acknowledges the significance of their bond with Jesus and the challenges they faced in navigating the transition from his physical presence to a spiritual connection.

Mary Magdalene's Comfort: Mary Magdalene's role in providing comfort to the grieving disciples showcases her empathetic nature and her deep understanding of the human experience. As a trusted confidante and disciple herself, Mary Magdalene's presence offers solace and support during a time of immense emotional turmoil.

Her ability to hold space for the disciples' grief and offer them comfort underscores her capacity for compassion and her role as a spiritual guide. Through her own experiences and insights, she offers the disciples a source of strength, reminding them of the transformative power of love and the enduring nature of their connection with Jesus.

Jesus' Encouragement: Jesus' words of encouragement in the Nag Hammadi texts serve as a beacon of hope and resilience for the grieving disciples. His reassurance that he is with them always, even in his physical absence, provides comfort and reinforces the eternal nature of their bond.

Jesus' encouragement acknowledges the disciples' pain and grief while urging them to embrace their spiritual connection and carry forward his teachings. His words remind them that they have the inner resources and the divine presence within to navigate the challenges they face, guiding them towards a sense of purpose and renewed commitment to their shared mission.

The Transformative Power of Love: The portrayal of Mary Magdalene's comfort and Jesus' encouragement within the Nag Hammadi texts underscores the transformative power of love in the face of grief and loss. Their presence and words offer a healing balm to the disciples, instilling them with hope, resilience, and a renewed sense of purpose.

Mary Magdalene's embodiment of compassion and Jesus' unwavering love provide the disciples with a foundation upon which to navigate their grief and continue their spiritual journey. Their messages convey the enduring nature of love and the transformative potential it holds to heal and uplift, even in the most challenging of circumstances.

Relevance in Today's World: The depiction of the disciples' grief and the comfort offered by Mary

Magdalene and Jesus resonate with the universal experience of loss and the need for support during times of emotional upheaval. Their teachings hold relevance in today's world, reminding us of the power of compassion, empathy, and spiritual connection to navigate periods of sorrow and uncertainty.

Mary Magdalene's role as a source of comfort and Jesus' words of encouragement inspire us to seek solace in the midst of grief, drawing upon our own capacity for love and resilience. Their example encourages us to support one another, embrace our spiritual connections, and find strength in the transformative power of love.

Conclusion: The portrayal of Mary Magdalene's comfort and Jesus' encouragement in the Nag Hammadi texts offers profound insights into the human experience of grief and the transformative power of love. Through their presence and words, they provide solace, hope, and a renewed sense of purpose for the disciples, guiding them through a time of immense emotional upheaval.

By reflecting upon their teachings and embodying their messages of compassion, empathy, and spiritual connection, we can find comfort and strength in the face of grief. Mary Magdalene's role as a comforting guide and Jesus' words of encouragement remind us of the enduring nature of love and the resilience of the human spirit, inspiring us to navigate our own challenges with grace, hope, and unwavering faith in the transformative power of love.

IV. The Vision of Mary

Mary's ascent and encounter with the Savior

In the Gospel of Mary, Mary undergoes a profound spiritual experience in which she ascends to a higher state of consciousness and encounters the Savior. She experiences a vision of the divine and receives a special revelation about the nature of the soul and the path to spiritual liberation.

During her ascent, Mary encounters a series of obstacles and challenges that test her faith and determination. She confronts demonic forces that seek to prevent her from reaching her destination, but she persists in her journey and ultimately overcomes these obstacles.

When Mary reaches the higher state of consciousness, she encounters the Savior, who reveals to her a secret teaching about the nature of the soul and the path to spiritual liberation. Mary receives this knowledge and is charged with sharing it with the other disciples.

Mary's ascent and encounter with the Savior illustrate the transformative power of spiritual practice and the potential for individuals to achieve higher states of consciousness and receive divine revelations.

Her experience highlights the importance of perseverance and determination in the face of spiritual obstacles, and underscores the value of sharing spiritual knowledge and insights with others.

Overall, Mary's ascent and encounter with the Savior provide a powerful testament to the potential for spiritual growth and enlightenment, and offer valuable insights into the nature of the spiritual journey.

Commentary:

Title: Mary Magdalene's Spiritual Ascension: A Profound Encounter with the Savior in the Nag Hammadi Texts

Introduction: Within the Nag Hammadi texts, a significant moment unfolds as Mary Magdalene embarks on a spiritual ascent and encounters the Savior. This commentary explores the depth of this encounter, delving into the themes of enlightenment, divine union, and the transformative power of personal revelation as depicted in the writings attributed to Mary Magdalene.

Mary's Ascension: Mary Magdalene's ascent in the Nag Hammadi texts symbolizes her journey of spiritual elevation and enlightenment. It represents her inner transformation, as she transcends the limitations of the physical realm and ascends to higher states of consciousness.

Her ascent serves as a metaphorical representation of the spiritual path, emphasizing the importance of personal growth, self-discovery, and the pursuit of divine knowledge. Mary's journey inspires seekers to embark on their own transformative quest, seeking a deeper connection with the divine and a profound understanding of their true nature.

Encounter with the Savior: Mary Magdalene's encounter with the Savior in the Nag Hammadi texts signifies the pinnacle of her spiritual journey. It represents a profound union with the divine, where she experiences a direct connection with the transcendent source of wisdom and love.

This encounter reflects the essential teachings attributed to Mary Magdalene, emphasizing the possibility of a direct and intimate relationship with the divine. It underscores the potential for personal revelation and the transformative power of encountering the divine presence within oneself.

The Transformative Power of Personal Revelation: The encounter between Mary Magdalene and the Savior in the Nag Hammadi texts illuminates the transformative power of personal revelation. It highlights the potential for profound inner awakening and the expansion of consciousness that occurs when individuals experience a direct connection with the divine.

Mary Magdalene's encounter with the Savior inspires seekers to embark on their own journeys of self-discovery and spiritual enlightenment. It encourages them to cultivate a deep sense of inner exploration, recognizing the divine spark within and the limitless potential for personal growth and transformation.

Relevance in Contemporary Spiritual Seekers: The depiction of Mary Magdalene's ascent and encounter with the Savior holds great relevance for contemporary spiritual seekers. It serves as a reminder of the inherent capacity within each individual to embark on a personal journey of enlightenment and encounter the divine within themselves.

Mary Magdalene's example invites us to transcend the limitations of external authorities and dogmas, embracing our own direct experiences of the divine. Her teachings remind us of the transformative power of personal revelation and the profound impact it can have on our lives, guiding us towards greater self-realization and a deepened connection with the sacred.

Conclusion: Mary Magdalene's ascent and encounter with the Savior in the Nag Hammadi texts offer profound insights into the transformative nature of spiritual awakening and the potential for a direct and intimate relationship with the divine. Her journey of enlightenment serves as an inspiration for contemporary seekers, encouraging them to embark on their own transformative quests and explore the depths of their spiritual potential.

By following Mary Magdalene's example and seeking personal revelation, we can cultivate a profound connection with the divine, experience inner transformation, and awaken to our true nature. Her teachings remind us that the path of spiritual ascension is available to all who seek it, offering the promise of enlightenment, divine union, and the transformative power of encountering the sacred within ourselves.

Mary's report to the disciples

In the Gospel of Mary, Mary reports to the other disciples about her ascent and encounter with the Savior. She shares with them the secret teaching that she received and urges them to pursue their own spiritual growth and liberation.

Mary's report to the disciples emphasizes the importance of sharing spiritual knowledge and insights with others. She recognizes that the journey to spiritual enlightenment is not a solitary one, and that individuals can benefit greatly from the support and guidance of others on the path.

Mary's report also highlights the value of personal experience and direct revelation in matters of faith. Rather than relying solely on the teachings of others, Mary encourages the disciples to seek out their own direct experiences of the divine and to trust their own intuition and inner guidance.

Overall, Mary's report to the disciples provides a powerful reminder of the importance of community and support in matters of faith, and underscores the value of personal experience and direct revelation in spiritual growth and enlightenment. Her words offer a call to action, urging the disciples to pursue their own spiritual journeys and share their insights and experiences with others.

Commentary:

Title: Mary Magdalene's Prophetic Message: Sharing the Revelation with the Disciples in the Nag Hammadi Texts

Introduction: In the Nag Hammadi texts, a significant moment unfolds as Mary Magdalene, having encountered profound revelations, shares her message with the disciples. This commentary explores the importance of Mary Magdalene's role as a bearer of divine knowledge, her courage to convey her insights, and the transformative impact of her report on the disciples' understanding of spiritual truth.

Mary's Encounter with Revelation: Mary Magdalene's encounter with revelation in the Nag

Hammadi texts signifies her deep spiritual insights and direct communion with divine wisdom. Her experience transcends conventional understanding, offering her profound insights into the nature of existence, the divine plan, and the purpose of human life.

Mary's report unveils her role as a prophetess, entrusted with transmitting divine revelations to the disciples. Her encounter underscores the significance of personal revelation and the potential for individuals to access higher knowledge through inner awakening and communion with the divine.

The Courage to Share: Mary Magdalene's report to the disciples demonstrates her courage and conviction in sharing the profound truths she has received. Despite potential skepticism or resistance from the disciples, she remains steadfast in her commitment to transmit the divine message entrusted to her.

Her courage highlights the importance of speaking one's truth and sharing spiritual insights, even when faced with skepticism or doubt. Mary's example encourages seekers to embrace their role as messengers of truth, trusting in the transformative power of their experiences and the potential impact on others' spiritual understanding.

The Transformative Impact: Mary Magdalene's report has a transformative impact on the disciples' understanding of spiritual truth. Her message challenges their existing beliefs, expands their consciousness, and invites them to explore deeper dimensions of spiritual reality.

The disciples' reception of Mary's report signifies their openness to receiving divine revelations and their willingness to question and expand their understanding. Mary's message inspires them to embark on their own inner journeys, seeking direct communion with the divine and embracing personal revelation as a means of spiritual growth and enlightenment.

Relevance in Contemporary Spirituality: Mary Magdalene's role as a transmitter of divine revelations in the Nag Hammadi texts holds great relevance in contemporary spirituality. It encourages individuals to trust their own spiritual experiences, listen to their inner wisdom, and share their insights with others.

Mary's example inspires seekers to move beyond dogmas and embrace the limitless potential of personal revelation. It emphasizes the importance of personal engagement with the divine, encouraging individuals to seek direct communion, explore profound insights, and share their transformative experiences to foster spiritual growth and collective understanding.

Conclusion: Mary Magdalene's report to the disciples in the Nag Hammadi texts highlights her role as a prophetess and the significance of her message in shaping the disciples' spiritual understanding. Her encounter with revelation and her courage to share it exemplify the power of personal revelation and the transformative impact it can have on individuals and communities.

Mary Magdalene's example encourages seekers to embrace their own spiritual insights, trust in their experiences, and convey their wisdom to others. Her teachings remind us of the profound nature of personal revelation and its potential to expand consciousness, challenge conventional beliefs, and foster spiritual growth. By embodying her example, we can deepen our own spiritual journey, contribute to the collective understanding of truth, and inspire others on their path to awakening.

The disciples' reaction and the end of the text

The Gospel of Mary describes the disciples' reaction to Mary's report about her ascent and encounter with the Savior. Some of the disciples express skepticism and doubt about her story, while others are more receptive and open to her message.

Peter, in particular, expresses his skepticism and challenges Mary's authority to teach the others. However, Andrew comes to Mary's defense, urging the disciples to listen to her words and consider their validity.

The Gospel of Mary ends abruptly, leaving the fate of the disciples and the future of their spiritual journey uncertain. However, the text emphasizes the importance of personal experience and direct revelation in matters of faith, and encourages readers to seek out their own spiritual insights and revelations.

Overall, the disciples' reaction and the end of the text highlight the challenges and complexities of the spiritual journey, and underscore the need for open-mindedness, discernment, and a willingness to seek out one's own spiritual experiences and insights.

Commentary:

Title: The Disciples' Response and the Enduring Legacy of Mary Magdalene in the Nag Hammadi Texts

Introduction: In the Nag Hammadi texts, Mary Magdalene's role as a central figure is evidenced by the disciples' reaction to her teachings and the lasting impact of her message. This commentary explores the disciples' response to Mary Magdalene's revelations and the significance of her enduring legacy, highlighting themes of spiritual authority, transformative learning, and the empowerment of women.

The Disciples' Reaction: The disciples' reaction to Mary Magdalene's teachings in the Nag Hammadi texts signifies a pivotal moment in their spiritual journey. Their response reveals both their receptiveness to her words and the transformative effect it has on their understanding of divine truth.

The disciples, initially skeptical or uncertain, gradually embrace the wisdom shared by Mary Magdalene. This shift reflects their willingness to challenge preconceived notions and open themselves to new perspectives. Their evolving acceptance highlights the transformative power of encountering a profound teacher and the expansion of consciousness that can result from embracing unconventional sources of spiritual guidance.

The Empowerment of Women: Mary Magdalene's role as a central figure in the Nag Hammadi texts challenges traditional gender roles and underscores the empowerment of women in matters of spirituality. Her presence as a spiritual authority demonstrates the importance of women's voices and contributions in the realm of divine knowledge.

By including Mary Magdalene as a prominent teacher and prophetess, the Nag Hammadi texts challenge patriarchal structures and elevate the role of women in spiritual leadership. This portrayal serves as a powerful statement of inclusivity, advocating for the recognition and empowerment of women within religious and spiritual contexts.

The Enduring Legacy: The portrayal of Mary Magdalene and the disciples' response in the Nag Hammadi texts establishes the enduring legacy of her teachings. Her message, transmitted through her encounters and reports, leaves an indelible mark on the disciples and subsequent generations of seekers.

Mary Magdalene's legacy extends beyond the confines of the text, inspiring individuals to embrace their spiritual authority, question societal norms, and seek direct communion with the divine. Her teachings resonate with contemporary audiences, providing a profound example of personal revelation, spiritual growth, and the transformative power of embracing one's inner wisdom.

Relevance in Contemporary Spirituality: The depiction of the disciples' response to Mary Magdalene's teachings holds relevance in contemporary spirituality. It calls upon individuals to critically evaluate established hierarchies and to embrace diverse perspectives, particularly those that have been historically marginalized.

Mary Magdalene's enduring legacy challenges prevailing narratives and invites seekers to recognize the inherent spiritual authority within themselves, regardless of gender or societal expectations. Her example encourages individuals to trust their own experiences, engage in transformative learning, and contribute to the ongoing evolution of spiritual understanding.

Conclusion: The disciples' reaction to Mary Magdalene's teachings and the enduring legacy of her message in the Nag Hammadi texts demonstrate the transformative power of encountering a spiritual authority who challenges existing norms. Mary Magdalene's presence as a prominent figure in these texts emphasizes the empowerment of women and invites seekers to embrace diverse sources of wisdom.

Her teachings continue to inspire individuals to question, learn, and grow in their spiritual journeys. By acknowledging and embracing the spiritual authority within ourselves, we can contribute to a more inclusive and expansive understanding of divine truth, following in the footsteps of Mary Magdalene and the disciples who recognized the profound value of her teachings.

Made in the USA
Monee, IL
03 February 2025

11450309R00066